Crocheted Wire & Bead JEWELRY

By Jacqui Harris

With additional projects
by
Debbie Baker
and
Basha Kooler

About the Designer

Social worker by day, jewelry designer by night, I began to crochet beaded necklaces about four years ago. Until then I had never even used a crochet hook but have been "hooked" ever since. I have made close to 500 necklaces, selling them at craft fairs and retail stores, or giving them as gifts to admiring friends. I've created one for every outfit and occasion! I want to give credit to my sister Debbie Baker whose Black Beauty design is on page 10. She had gone to a class to make wire beaded bracelets and was disappointed with the finished product. Using her experience with crocheting, Debbie came up with a finished product that looked like fine jewelry using three or sometimes as many as nine crocheted strands braided together. My passion for jewelry (inherited from my father who is a jeweler) and some talent in design led to the various patterns and variations for the different projects. I hope to share the technique with anyone who likes to do something fairly simple and have it look quite fantastic. The best part of all is that every necklace is made from the same basic crochet stitch. The patterns are produced by the order of the beads on the wire and where the beads fall when braiding the strands. I recommend reading through the basic instructions first, so you'll have an idea of how one step leads to the next, then you can take off and create your own fabulous necklace designs. I've never had a hobby that fires my imagination as much as this and also pays for itself. For this I am grateful to Debbie who showed me "how to." Now you can learn how, too. ENJOY!

Jacqui Harris

This book is dedicated to my father, Herbert Harris, who always dreamed of seeing the family name in print.
Acknowledgements:To my sister, Debbie, without whom there would be no necklaces.
To my dearest friend, Linnea, without whom there would be no book.
To my husband, Jeff, whose support, patience, and humor keeps me going no matter what.

CONTENTS

GENERAL INFORMATION

NOTE: Many of the photos in this book are enlarged to show the project in detail. Refer to finished measurements on project instructions for actual size.

GAUGE

The size of the crochet hook, the gauge of the wire, the size of the beads, and how tightly you make your stitches will determine the gauge of your project. For the projects in this book, use a G (4.00mm) or H (5.00mm) aluminum crochet hook to obtain a gauge of 4 stitches per inch. Make a sample chain using both hook sizes to check your gauge.

TOOLS

Be sure to use a metal crochet hook when working with wire. You will need flat-nose pliers (preferably 2 pairs), round-nose pliers, and any small gauge wire cutters. A large needle or an awl for opening finishing loops is useful, as well as a long ruler for measuring strands. A bead board that has compartments and space to lay out your beads can give you an idea of how they will look as a necklace before you load the beads onto the wire.

MATERIALS

BEADS

Beads come in every size, shape and color imaginable. (See Resources, page 36.) Choose from crystals, pearls or semi-precious gems. Use round, faceted, drop, square-cut or briolette shapes. Combine tiny seed pearls with 18mm crystals for drama and elegance. You can add to your bead collection by taking apart old jewelry or removing the beads from an old garment or pillow.

WIRE

Beading wire is available in many gauges—the lower the gauge number the thicker the wire. Twenty-eight gauge wire works well for crochet jewelry due to its great flexibility. It is available on spools containing about 40 yards of wire in gold tone, silver tone, gold plated, sterling silver and various colors.

CLASPS AND FINDINGS

Finishing your necklace with a complementary clasp is a must. Many clasps are available including toggle, lobster claw, magnetic, and "S" clasps used in combination with jump rings and cones (see photo of matched sets, right). A variety of barrel beads with larger holes to accommodate and hide your twisted wire ends are also available. Balance the weight of the clasp with that of the necklace (i.e., for a heavier necklace use a heavier clasp and findings).

GENERAL INSTRUCTIONS

All of the necklaces in this book are made exactly the same way by crocheting and braiding the strands. The only differences are in the number of strands you use, the sequence you use when loading the beads, and how the beads lay in patterns when braided. Create all the projects in this book using a simple crochet chain stitch and beaded chain stitch.

BASIC CROCHET CHAIN STITCH

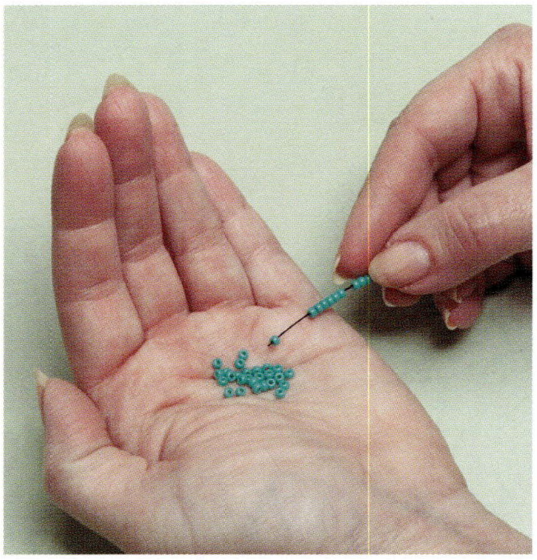

1 Load required number of beads onto the wire spool.

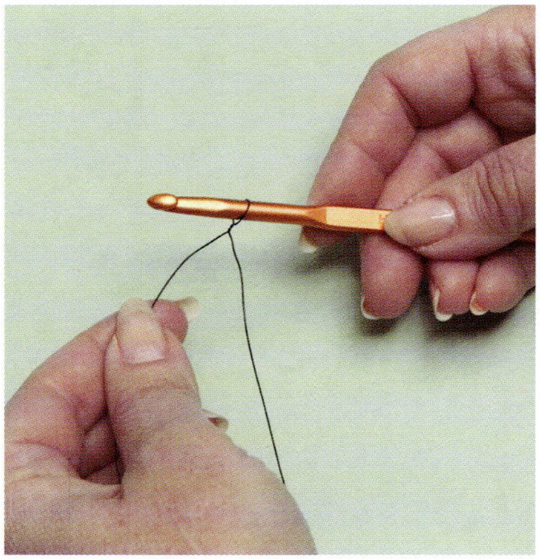

2 Start the chain stitch with a slip knot or fold end of wire across flat part of crochet hook, pinch wires together close to hook, and twist 2–3 times to create the first loop. Leave a 3" tail.

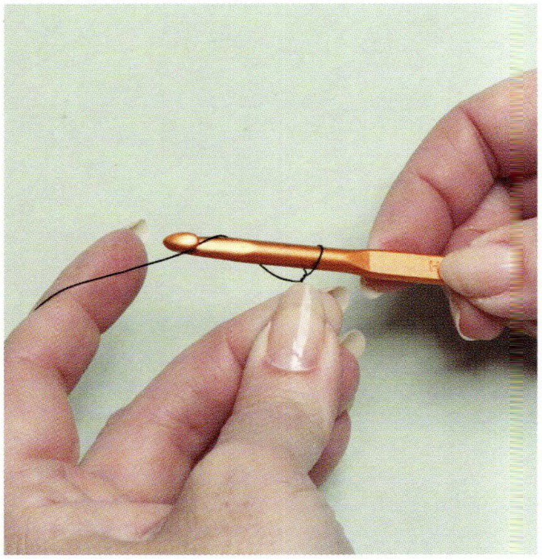

3 Guide long wire over hook and pull wire through loop. Make two chain stitches before the first beaded chain stitch.

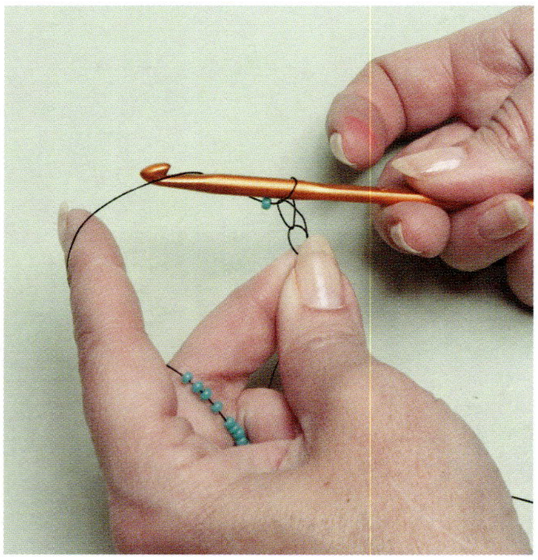

4 For the beaded chain stitch, slide bead up to the chain then guide long wire over hook.

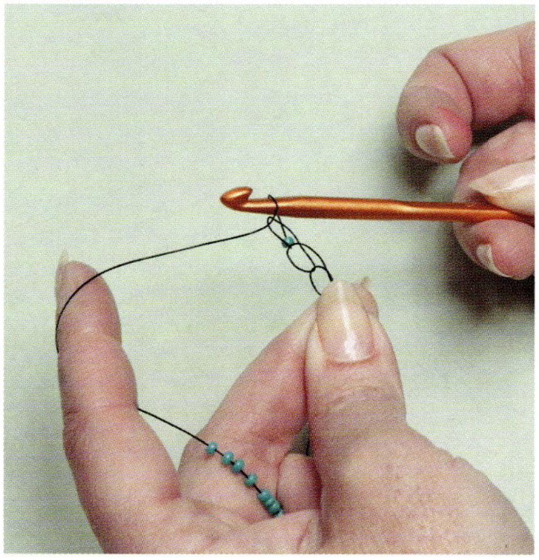

5 Pull wire through to complete the chain.

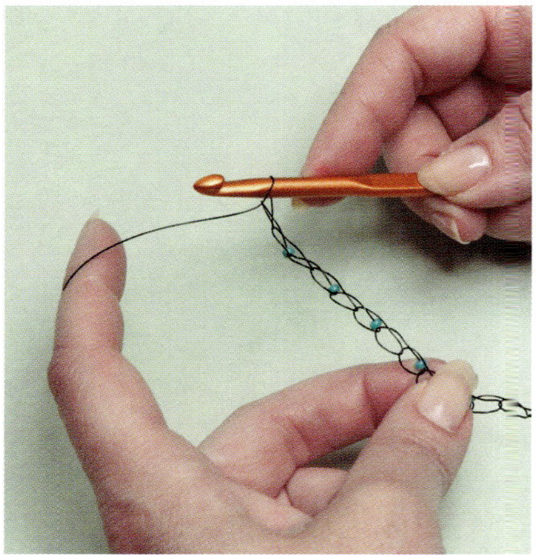

6 Continue pattern to desired strand length. Finish with 2 chain stitches after last bead. Cut wire, leaving 3" tail, then pull through last loop.

BRAIDING

All the braiding in this book is based on three-section braiding. The number of strands included in each section is determined by the pattern of the necklace. Braiding examples are: 1–1–1, 2–1–2, 2–2–2, 3–1–3, 3–3–3 etc.

Instructions for each pattern indicate when to braid single strands or a group of strands (section) together before final braiding. NOTE: Braiding each section before final braiding will make a shorter wider necklace. The example below shows 1–1–1 braiding.

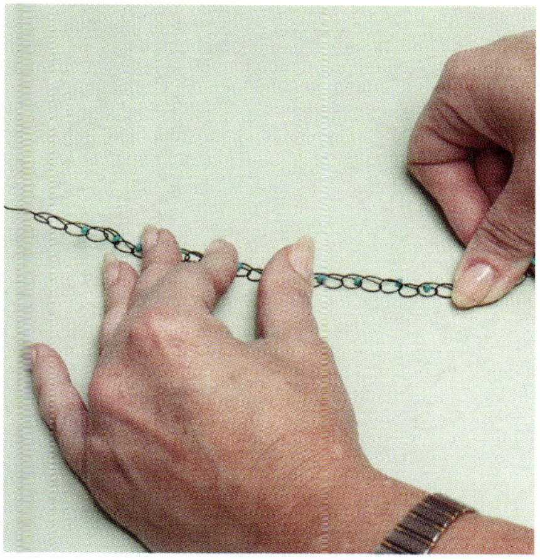

1 Lay the strands flat and gently straighten. All strands should be the same length before braiding.

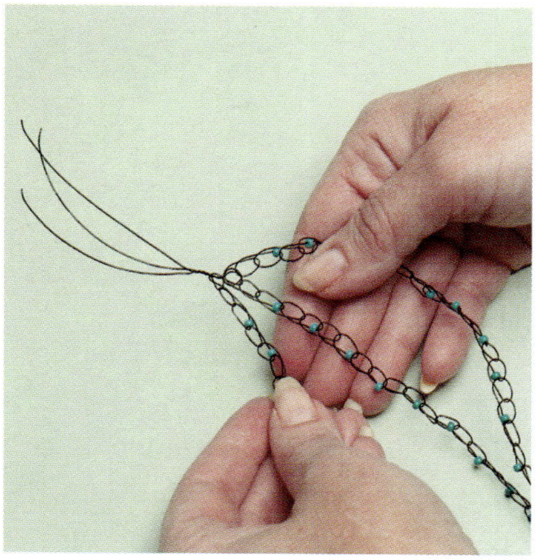

2 Hold three strands together above the first chain. Pinch the wires and tightly twist 2-3 times.

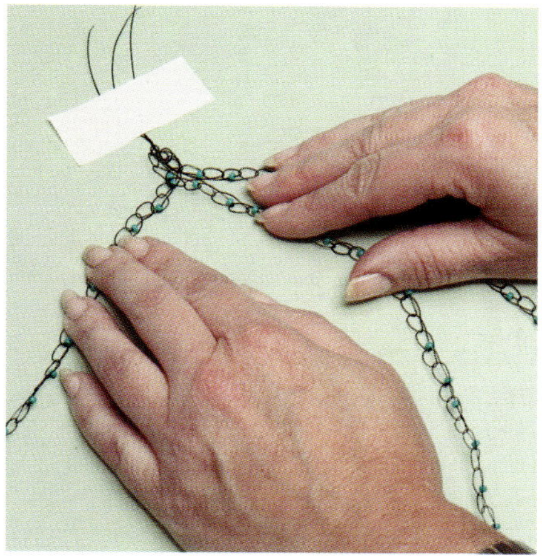

3 Use tape or a clip to secure the twisted end to a flat surface.

4 Braid together, alternating right and left over center strand and making sure your strands stay flat and your braid stays straight. Use your fingers to push larger beads to the front of the necklace.

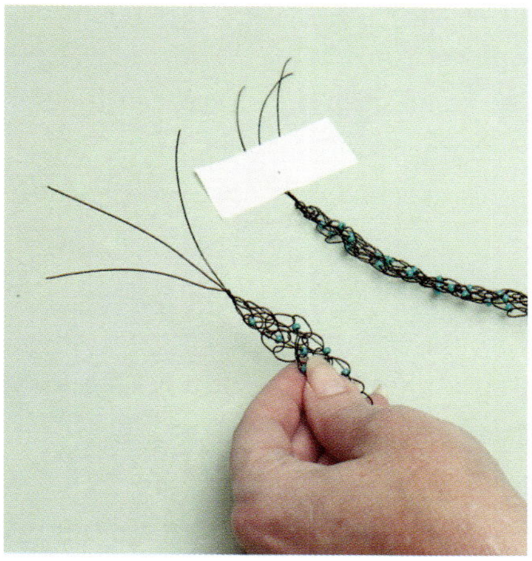

5 After braiding twist the ends of the wire together as in step 2. Then continue twisting the three wires to make a single wire. Twist the other end into a single wire also. Note: When braiding multiple sections, twist loose wire ends into one wire after all sections are combined.

Necklace Lengths and Styles

Many of the necklaces in this book are choker or princess length but can be adapted to any length you wish. Enjoy trying some other styles.

Collar: 12–13 inches, multiple strands worn snugly around the neck like a dog collar.

Choker: 14–16 inches, sits just above the collarbone.

Princess: 17–19 inches, looks great with higher necklines.

Matinee: 20–23 inches, a little longer for casual or chic looks.

Opera: 28–34 inches, can be doubled into a choker.

Rope: 40–45 inches, versatile for many looks.

Lariat: 48 inches or more, with ends left unattached for knotting or wrapping around the neck.

FINISHING

1 Fold the twisted end in half, leaving twice enough wire to accommodate your finishing bead or cone and a small loop. Twist once around the wire to secure and make a loop. Use pliers to pinch the loop nearly flat to fit through the finishing bead.

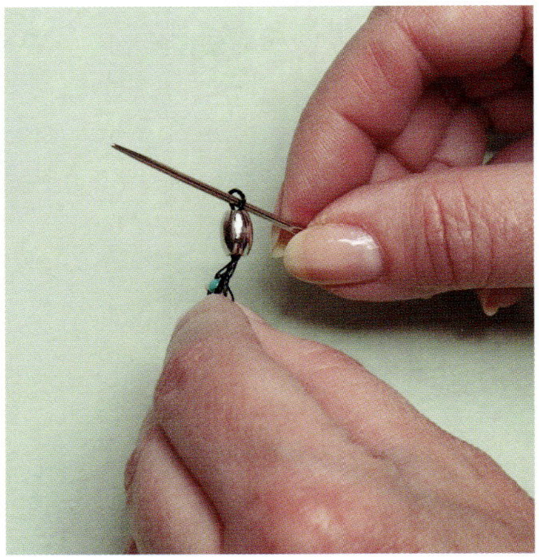

2 Thread the wire through a finishing bead or cone, leaving the folded end exposed. Use a large needle or awl to open the folded end into a loop. Repeat steps 1–3 on the other end.

3 Finish by adding a jump ring and clasp of your choice (see page 5 for clasp ideas).

TIPS

• Crocheted necklaces can be created in a small work space which makes them very portable. Before transporting, count and load the beads on a spool at home, roll up into a re-sealable plastic bag, and you're ready to stitch anywhere you would be comfortable knitting or crocheting.

• Determine which side of your completed necklace looks best for the "front." The side showing more of the wire and less of the beads should be the back. When braiding try to lay the beads so that they "pop out" on top by pulling any beads forward that may fall behind the braiding.

• Shaping is important so the necklace will lay flat against your throat. Lay the completed necklace on a flat surface. Using the palm of your hand, press the necklace flat in the shape of an open "U".

• Shape your necklace to fit your mood. If you want to make a choker, manipulate the wire so that the necklace stands on its side. When you want the necklace to lay down flat again around your neck, just coax the wires back into "U" position.

• "Scrunch" a necklace to make it shorter, wider and lacier. Lay it flat and carefully push the ends toward the center, scrunching every few inches or so.

• Give a curved convex shape to wider necklaces containing 5, 7, or 9 braided strands. Place your straightened index finger on the back of the necklace; bend the necklace over your finger, pressing the upper and lower edges against the length of your finger to create a soft curve.

• Many of these necklaces can also be worn as a bracelet by wrapping two or three times around the wrist. They also look lovely as a headband or hair wreath for a flower girl in a wedding party; just match the bridal colors with the beads.

• Before braiding strands together, try holding each end of the finished strand and giving a hard tug. This will lengthen and flatten the stitches and create a different look. (For an example, see the Grapevine variation on page 34)

Bejeweled

By Jacqui Harris
Finished necklace 1"x15"

MATERIALS

228 assorted beads and pearls
18 yards of 28 gauge gold wire
Size H (5.00mm) aluminum crochet hook or size needed to obtain a gauge of 4 chains = 1"
2 barrel beads
2 jump rings
Clasp
Tools (see page 4)

INSTRUCTIONS

6 strands braided 2–2–2

Refer to Basic Crochet Chain instructions, page 6. Strands 1–6: For each strand load gold wire with 38 assorted beads. Crochet chain, adding bead every other stitch.

BRAIDING

Each strand will be approximately 18" before braiding. Separate the 6 strands into three pairs and braid (see Braiding, page 7).

FINISHING

Attach finishing beads, jump rings, and clasp (see Finishing, page 8).

DESIGN PATTERNS

Now that you know how to make a basic crocheted wire necklace, it's easy to create several different patterns to achieve different effects. All of the projects in this book are grouped into these patterns produced by the order of the beads on the wire and where the beads fall when braiding the strands. But don't be afraid to break the rules and create your own unique designs.

RANDOM

The random pattern is for the free spirit in all of us. Just pick your favorite colors, shapes, and sizes of beads, and you're good to go. Whether you add a bead to every stitch or every other stitch, the possibilities are endless and the results spectacular.

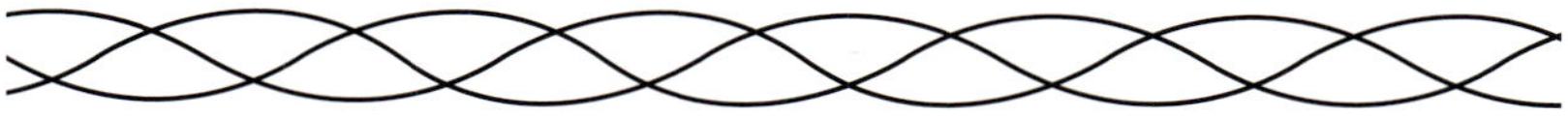

Random 10

Black Beauty

By Debbie Baker
Finished necklace 1"x15"

MATERIALS

342 assorted beads
27 yards of 28 gauge black wire
Size H (5.00mm) aluminum crochet hook or
size needed to obtain gauge of 4 chains = 1"
2 barrel beads
2 jump rings
Clasp
Tools (see page 4)

INSTRUCTIONS

9 strands braided 3–3–3

Refer to Basic Crochet Chain instructions, page 6.
Strands 1–9: For each strand load black wire with 38 assorted beads. Crochet chain, adding a bead every other stitch.

BRAIDING

Each strand will be approximately 18" before braiding the 3 sections, braid each section then braid the 3 braided sections into one big braid. (see Braiding, page 7).

FINISHING

Attach finishing beads, jump rings, and clasp (see Finishing, page 8).

Purple Passion

By Debbie Baker
Finished necklace ¾"x15"

MATERIALS

228 assorted shapes and shades of lavender beads
1 lavender quartz heart
18 yards of 28 gauge lavender wire
Size H (5.00mm) aluminum crochet hook or size needed to obtain gauge of 4 chains = 1"
2 barrel beads
3 jump rings
Clasp
Tools (see page 4)

INSTRUCTIONS

6 strands braided 2–2–2

Refer to Basic Crochet Chain instructions, page 6. Strands 1–6: For each strand load lavender wire with 38 assorted beads. Crochet chain, adding bead every other stitch.

BRAIDING

Each strand will be approximately 18" before braiding. Separate 6 strands into 3 pairs and braid (see Braiding, page 7).

FINISHING

Attach finishing beads, jump rings, and clasp (see Finishing, page 8).

EMBELLISHMENT

Using jump ring, attach lavender quartz heart at midpoint of necklace (refer to photo).

The Mermaid

By Jacqui Harris
Finished necklace 1"x16"

MATERIALS

60 (5mm) pearls
96 silver hex beads
34 (8mm) amazonite faceted beads
15 yards of 28 gauge copper wire
Size H (5.00mm) aluminum crochet hook or size needed to obtain gauge of 4 chains = 1"
2 barrel beads
2 jump rings
Clasp
Tools (see page 4)

INSTRUCTIONS

5 strands braided 2–1–2

Refer to Basic Crochet Chain instructions, page 6. Strands 1–3: For each strand load copper wire, alternating 20 pearl and 20 hex beads. Crochet chain, adding bead every other stitch. Strands 4–5: For each strand load wire, alternating 17 hex beads and 17 faceted beads, ending with a hex bead. Crochet chain, adding bead every other stitch.

BRAIDING

Each strand will be approximately 19" before braiding. Separate into 2 pairs (a pearl strand and faceted strand in each pair) and a single pearl strand. Braid together in no special order (see Braiding, page 7).

FINISHING

Attach finishing beads, jump rings, and clasp (see Finishing, page 8).

RIBBON

The ribbon design incorporates an unstitched strand of solid beads or pearls braided into the design. The ribbon is a distinctive variation for your crocheted necklace. It can be basic or, by adding an accent bead such as a charm or briolette, it can add whimsy or drama. It gives an impression of a wave flowing through your necklace. For a basic ribbon, cut a length of wire as long as your finished crocheted strand. Make a knot 3" from the end (or a double knot if your bead holes are large). Knot again after loading beads.

Juliet's

By Jacqui Harris

Finished necklace ⅝"x16"

MATERIALS

60 honey-colored triangle beads
20 lavender crystal beads
Cream-colored pearl seed beads
12 yards of 28 gauge gold wire
Size H (5.00mm) aluminum crochet hook or size needed to obtain gauge of 4 chains = 1"
2 barrel beads
2 jump rings
Clasp
Tools (see page 4)

INSTRUCTIONS

3 strands, 2 ribbons braided 2–1–2

Refer to Basic Crochet Chain instructions, page 6. Strands 1–2: For each strand load gold wire with 40 honey-colored triangle beads. Crochet chain, adding bead every other stitch. Strand 3: Load wire with 20 honey triangle beads, alternating with 20 lavender beads. Crochet chain, adding bead every other stitch. For ribbons load 2 strands of pearl seed beads, matching the same length as your crocheted strands. NOTE: number of beads varies according to the size of the seed bead.

BRAIDING

Strands will be approx. 18" before braiding. Add a ribbon to the inside of the left strand and inside of the right strand and braid as usual (see Braiding, page 7).

FINISHING

Attach finishing beads, jump rings, and clasp (see Finishing, page 8).

Ocean Beach

By Jacqui Harris
Finished necklace ¾"x18"

MATERIALS

28 medium aqua crystal beads
28 medium green crystal beads
48 small iridescent beads
11 (7mm) apple green small crystal beads
10 (5mm) dark turquoise small crystal beads
280 white seed beads or enough to fill 20" of wire
10 yards of 28 gauge silver wire
Size H (5.00mm) aluminum crochet hook or size needed to obtain gauge of 4 chains = 1"
2 barrel beads
2 jump rings
Clasp
Tools (see page 4)

INSTRUCTIONS

3 strands, 1 ribbon braided 1–1–2

Refer to Basic Crochet Chain instructions, page 6. Strands 1–2: For each strand load silver wire with 14 large aqua crystal beads, alternating with 14 large green crystal beads and 14 medium iridescent beads. Crochet chain, adding bead every other stitch. Strand 3: Load wire with medium apple green crystal beads, medium dark turquoise crystal beads, and medium iridescent beads in the following sequence: iridescent, green, iridescent, turquoise, etc. Crochet chain, adding bead every other stitch. For the ribbon, load wire with about 20" white seed beads matching same length as other strands.

BRAIDING

Strands will be approx. 20" before braiding. Add the ribbon to the strand on the right and braiding them as one strand (see Braiding, page 7).

FINISHING

Attach finishing beads, jump rings, and clasp (see Finishing, page 8).

Real Rich

By Jacqui Harris
Finished necklace ⅞"x15"

MATERIALS

78 brown quartz beads
78 pale pink quartz beads
Approximately 378 iridescent brown seed beads
22 yards of 28 gauge gold wire
Size H (5.00mm) aluminum crochet hook or size needed to obtain gauge of 4 chains = 1"
2 barrel beads
2 jump rings
Clasp
Tools (see page 4)

INSTRUCTIONS

6 strands, 1 ribbon braided 3–1–3

Refer to Basic Crochet Chain instructions, page 6. Strands 1–6: For each strand load wire with 13 beads each of brown seed bead, brown quartz, pale pink quartz in that sequence. Crochet chain, adding a bead every other stitch. For ribbon strand, load wire with approximately 378 iridescent seed beads, matching the same length as your crocheted strands. NOTE: number of beads varies according to the size of the seed bead.

BRAIDING

Strands will be approx. 18" before braiding. Divide crocheted strands into 2 sections, then braid the 3 strands in each section. Add the ribbon strand on the right for one more section then braid all 3 sections together (see Braiding, page 7).

FINISHING

Attach finishing beads, jump rings, and clasp (see Finishing, page 8).

Biwa Baby

By Jacqui Harris
Finished necklace ⅝"x14"

MATERIALS

68 copper mirrored beads
30 large Biwa pearls
3 yards of 28 gauge silver wire
6 yards of 28 gauge copper wire
Size H (5.00mm) aluminum crochet hook or
size needed to obtain gauge of 4 chains = 1"
2 barrel beads
2 jump rings
Clasp
Tools (see page 4)

NOTE: This ribbon is made of large gray Biwa pearls crocheted on silver wire which makes the pearls look like they're floating.

INSTRUCTIONS

3 strands braided 1–1–1

Refer to Basic Crochet Chain instructions, page 6. Strands 1–2: For each strand load copper wire with 34 copper mirrored beads. Crochet chain, adding bead every other stitch. For the ribbon strand, load silver wire with 30 large biwa pearls. Crochet chain, adding bead every other stitch.

BRAIDING

Strands will be approx. 16" before braiding. Braid 3 strands together (see Braiding, page 7).

FINISHING

Attach finishing beads, jump rings, and clasp (see Finishing, page 8).

Pearl Fantasy

By Basha Kooler

Finished necklace 1¼"x24"

MATERIALS

18 pink faceted crystal beads
18 smoke gray faceted crystal beads
168 pearls in assorted sizes and colors
120 ivory (3mm) pearls
120 white (3mm) pearls
20 yards of 28 gauge silver wire
25 yards of 28 gauge copper wire
Size H (5.00mm) aluminum crochet hook
  or size needed to obtain gauge of
  4 chains = 1"
2 barrel beads
2 jump rings
Clasp
Tools (see page 4)

INSTRUCTIONS

9 strands braided 3–3–3

Refer to Basic Crochet Chain instructions, page 6. Strands 1–2: crochet silver wire until each strand measures 28". Strand 3: Load wire, alternating 18 pink and 18 smoke gray crystals. Crochet chain, adding bead every other stitch. Strands 4–6: For each strand load copper wire with 56 pearls in assorted sizes and colors. Crochet strand, adding bead every other stitch. Strands 7–8: Combine 1 silver wire and 1 copper wire and crochet until each strand measures 28". Ribbon strand 9: Load copper wire, alternating 120 ivory and 120 white (3mm) pearls, matching same length as other strands.

BRAIDING

Strands will be approx. 28" before braiding. Divide strands into 3 sections (section 1 = strands 1–3, section 2 = strands 4–6, section 3 = strands 7–9). Braid strands in each section loosely then braid sections, keeping section 3 on the right for a nice wavy look (see Braiding, page 7).

FINISHING

Attach finishing beads, jump rings, and clasp (see Finishing, page 8).

The Opera

By Jacqui Harris
Finished necklace ⅝"x32"

MATERIALS

84 aqua mirrored triangle beads
84 champagne mirrored triangle beads
84 dark gray mirrored beads
148 pearls
147 silver seed beads
15 yards of 28 gauge copper wire
Size H (5.00mm) aluminum crochet hook or size needed to obtain gauge of 4 chains = 1"
2 barrel beads
2 jump rings
Clasp
Tools (see page 4)

INSTRUCTIONS

3 strands, 1 ribbon 1–1–2

Refer to Basic Crochet Chain instructions, page 6. Strand 1: Load copper wire with 84 champagne mirrored triangle beads. Crochet chain, adding bead every other stitch. Repeat with dark gray and aqua beads for strands 2–3. For ribbon strand 4: Load wire, alternating approx. 148 pearls and 147 silver seed beads, ending with a pearl and matching length of other strands.

BRAIDING

Strands will be approx. 34" before braiding. Place aqua strand on right and combine with ribbon strand then braid all together (see Braiding, page 7).

FINISHING

Attach finishing beads, jump rings, and clasp (see Finishing, page 8).

ZIGZAG

It's obvious why this is called a zigzag pattern; it's just a ribbon or strand that was straightened out between large accent beads so that they fall on the outer edges of the necklace. If you think it would look better wavy and loose, try it.

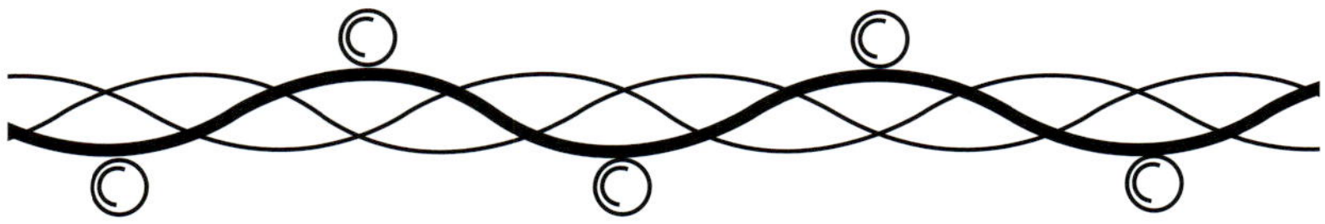

Spring Garden

By Jacqui Harris
Finished necklace ⅝"x15"

MATERIALS

72 small green beads
144 white seed beads
90 (4mm) rose quartz beads
17 (5mm) pink Swarovski beads
9 yards of 28 gauge silver wire
Size H (5.00mm) aluminum crochet hook or size needed to obtain gauge of 4 chains = 1"
2 jump rings
2 barrel beads
Clasp
Tools (see page 4)

INSTRUCTIONS

3 strands braided 1–1–1

Refer to Basic Crochet Chain instructions, page 6. Load silver wire to make 1 ribbon strand, alternating 5 rose quartz beads and 1 pink Swarovski bead 17 times, ending with 5 rose quartz beads. Strands 2–3: For each strand load wire, alternating 2 white beads and a single green bead 36 times. Crochet chain, alternating stitches with 2 white beads then a green bead. Beads on every other stitch.

BRAIDING

Strands will be approx. 18" before braiding. Braid the 3 strands with the ribbon strand starting on the right, coupled with a strand making sure the pink Swarovski beads fall on the outer edge, alternating right and left side (see Braiding, page 7).

FINISHING

Attach finishing beads, jump rings, and clasp (see Finishing, page 8).

Amber Galaxy

By Basha Kooler
Finished necklace 1¼"x19"

MATERIALS

111 Small pearls
9 large amber faceted crystal beads
30 medium amber faceted crystal beads
9 large clear faceted crystal beads
65 small clear faceted crystal beads
25 yards of 28 gauge copper wire
Size H (5.00mm) aluminum crochet hook or size needed to obtain gauge of 4 chains = 1"
2 jump rings
2 barrel beads
Clasp
Tools (see page 4)

INSTRUCTIONS

9 strands braided 3-3-3

Strands 1–3: Using copper wire, crochet 3 strands of chains 22" long. Strands 4–6: For each strand load copper wire with 37 pearls. Crochet chain, adding bead every other stitch. Strand 7: Load wire, alternating small clear beads and medium amber beads for a total of 20 beads of each color. Crochet chain, adding a bead every other stitch. Strand 8: Load wire with 3 small clear beads and a large clear bead repeated 9 times and ending with 3 small clear beads. Crochet chain, adding bead every other stitch. Load wire for Strand 9 as follows: small clear bead, medium. amber bead, small clear bead, large amber bead. Repeat 9 times, ending with a clear bead, medium. amber bead and a small clear bead. Crochet chain, adding bead every other stitch.

BRAIDING

All strands should be approximately 22" before braiding. Divide strands into 3 sections (section 1 = strands 1–3, section 2 = strands 4–6, section 3 = strands 7–9). Braid the 3 strands in each section. Finish by braiding the three sections together with the large beads falling to the right and left sides of the necklace in a zigzag pattern (see Braiding, page 7).

FINISHING

Attach finishing beads, jump rings, and clasp (see Finishing, page 8).

Palm Beach

By Jacqui Harris
Finished necklace 1"x18"

MATERIALS

15 (8mm) amazonite faceted beads
76 honey faceted Swarovski beads
136 white beads
136 gold metallic seed beads
76 gold colored glass
16 yards of 28 gauge copper wire
Size H (5.00mm) aluminum crochet hook or size needed to obtain gauge of 4 chains = 1"
2 jump rings
2 barrel beads
Clasp
Tools (see page 4)

INSTRUCTIONS

5 strands braided 2–2–1

Strands 1–2: For each strand load gold wire alternating one each of 30 honey faceted Swarovski beads, 30 white beads, and 30 gold seed beads. Crochet chain, adding bead every other stitch. Strands 3–4: For each strand load wire alternating one each of 30 gold beads, 30 white beads, 30 gold seed beads. Crochet chain, adding a bead to each stitch. Strand 5: Load wire with white bead, honey faceted bead, gold seed bead, 8mm amazonite bead, 15 times, ending with white bead, honey bead, gold seed bead. Crochet chain, adding a bead to each stitch.

BRAIDING

All strands will be approx. 20" before braiding. Divide strands into 3 sections (section 1 = strands 1 and 3, section 2 = strands 2 and 4, section 3 = strand 5). Braid with strand 5 on the right, making sure the large amazonite beads fall on the outer edge, alternating right and left sides (see Braiding, page 7).

FINISHING

Attach finishing beads, jump rings, and clasp (see Finishing, page 8).

Lavender Ice

By Jacqui Harris
Finished necklace 5/8"x15"

MATERIALS

39 tanzanite crystal beads
18 (5mm) lime crystal beads
18 peach crystal beads
22 (2mm) pearls
7 pink crystal cubes
9 yards of 28 gauge magenta wire
Size H (5.00mm) aluminum crochet hook
or size needed to obtain gauge
of 4 chains = 1"
2 barrel beads
2 jump rings
Clasp
Tools (see page 4)

INSTRUCTIONS

3 strands braided 1–1–1

Strand 1: Load magenta wire, alternating 18 peach and 18 tanzanite crystals. Crochet chain, adding bead every other stitch. Strand 2: Load wire, alternating 18 pearls and 18 lime crystals. Crochet chain, adding bead every other stitch. Strand 3: Load wire with two pearls. Then alternate 3 tanzanite crystals and 1 pink crystal cube, repeating 7 times, ending with 3 tanzanite crystals and 2 more pearls. Crochet chain, adding bead every other stitch.

BRAIDING

NOTE: Strands will be approx. 18" before braiding. Braid the 3 strands together with strand 3 starting on the right, making sure that the cube beads fall on the outer right side of the braid (see Braiding, page 7).

FINISHING

Attach finishing beads, jump rings, and clasp (see Finishing, page 8).

DANGLES

Dangling beads add new dimension and detail to the basic braided necklace. Just load the beads as described and braid with the dangling beaded strand on the right. Braid so that the dangles fall on the right side of the braid for a "drop bead" look. Use charms, or any other drop bead for a different look.

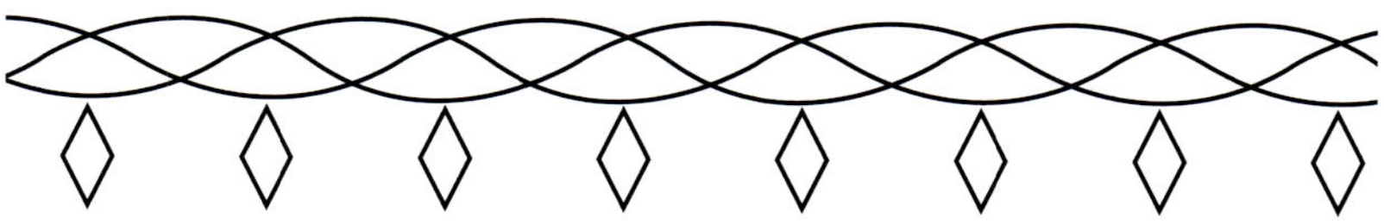

Art Deco

By Jacqui Harris
Finished necklace ½"x14"

MATERIALS

34 black hex beads
290 black seed beads
129 honey-colored seed beads
7 honey-colored crystal briolette drops
9 yards of 28 gauge black wire
Size H (5.00mm) aluminum crochet hook or size needed to obtain gauge of 4 chains = 1"
2 barrel beads
2 jump rings
Clasp
Tools (see page 4)

INSTRUCTIONS

3 strands braided 1–1–1

Strand 1: Load black wire with 34 hex beads. Crochet chain, adding bead every other stitch. Strand 2: Load wire with 129 honey-colored seed beads. Crochet chain, adding 3 seed beads to a stitch at every other stitch. For ribbon strand 3 load wire as follows: 55 black seed beads, then 1 briolette, 30 black seed beads 6 times ending with 1 briolette and 55 black seed beads.

BRAIDING

NOTE: Strands will be approximately 18" before braiding. Braid the 3 strands with the ribbon on the right making briolettes fall along the right edge of the necklace (see Braiding, page 7).

FINISHING

Attach finishing beads, jump rings, and clasp (see Finishing, page 8).

Pink Daisies

By Jacqui Harris
Finished necklace ½"x13"

MATERIALS

53 pink crystal beads
24 lavender crystal beads
5 flower beads
9 yards of 28 gauge magenta wire
Size H (5.00mm) aluminum crochet hook or size needed to obtain gauge of 4 chains = 1"
2 barrel beads
2 jump rings
Clasp
Tools (see page 4)

INSTRUCTIONS

3 strands braided 1–1–1

Strands 1–2: For each strand load magenta wire with 29 pink crystal beads. Crochet chain, adding bead every other stitch. Strand 3: Load wire, alternating 4 lavender crystal beads and 1 flower bead, repeating 5 times and ending with 4 pink crystal beads. Crochet chain, adding bead every other stitch and adding extra stitch for each flower bead.

BRAIDING

Strands will be approx. 16" before braiding. Braid the 3 strands with flower strand on the right, making the flowers fall along the right edge (see Braiding, page 7).

FINISHING

Attach finishing beads, jump rings, and clasp (see Finishing, page 8).

Little Princess

By Jacqui Harris
Finished necklace ½"x13"

MATERIALS

92 assorted pastel pearlized beads
3 pewter charms
9 yards of 28 gauge silver wire
Size H (5.00mm) aluminum crochet hook
or size needed to obtain gauge
4 chains = 1"
2 barrel beads
2 jump rings
Clasp
Tools (see page 4)

INSTRUCTIONS

3 strands braided 1–1–1

Strands 1–2: For each strand load silver wire with 32 beads randomly. Crochet chain, adding bead every other stitch. For strand 3, load wire in the following sequence: 12 beads, 1 charm, 2 beads, 1 charm, 2 beads, 1 charm, ending with 12 beads. Crochet chain, adding bead every other stitch.

BRAIDING

Strands will be approx. 16" before braiding. Braid the 3 strands with charm strand on the right so charms will fall along the right edge (see Braiding, page 7).

FINISHING

Attach finishing beads, jump rings, and clasp (see Finishing, page 8).

Coronation

By Jacqui Harris
Finished necklace ¾"x15"

MATERIALS

14 (4mm) clear crystal beads
7 (3mm) emerald green crystal beads
6 (8mm) emerald green crystal beads
152 (2mm) pearls
372 gold-tone seed beads
15 yards of 28 gauge gold wire
Size H (5.00mm) aluminum crochet hook or size needed to obtain gauge of 4 chains = 1"
2 barrel beads
2 jump rings
Clasp

INSTRUCTIONS

5 strands braided 2–2–1

Strands 1–4: For each strand load wire alternating 2 gold-tone seed beads and 1 pearl, repeating 38 times and ending with 2 gold-tone seed beads. Crochet chain, adding 1 pearl or 2 gold beads every stitch. Strand 5: Load wire with 2 gold beads, 1 clear crystal bead, 2 gold beads, 1 (3mm) green crystal, 2 gold beads, 1 clear crystal bead, 2 gold beads, 1 (8mm) green crystal bead) 6 times, 2 gold, 1 crystal bead, 2 gold beads, 1 (3mm) green crystal bead, 2 gold beads. Crochet chain, adding a single bead at every stitch.

BRAIDING

Strands will be approx. 18" before braiding. Make 2 pairs with the pearls and gold seed beads strands. Place the strands with the crystals on the right and braid them together so that the clear beads "pop up" in the center of the braid (see Braiding, page 7).

FINISHING

Attach finishing beads, jump rings, and clasp (see Finishing, page 8).

CENTER POP

This pattern shows the main accent beads as a focal point in the middle of the braid. What's different here is the way you load the beads on the wire. It will braid itself into this pattern. The center pop style also makes lovely head bands.

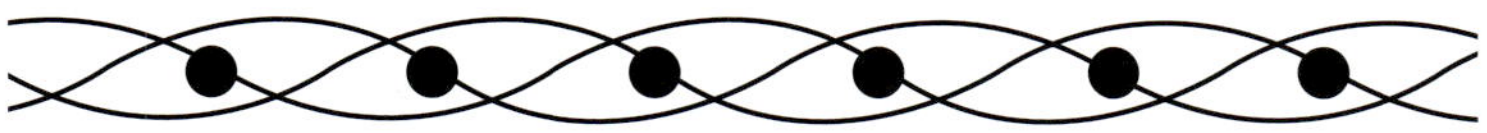

Cranberry Rose

By Jacqui Harris
Finished necklace ¾"x15"

MATERIALS

340 red bugle beads
11 clear crystal beads
15 yards of 28 gauge copper wire
Size H (5.00mm) aluminum crochet hook or size needed to obtain gauge of 4 chains = 1"
2 barrel beads
2 jump rings
Clasp
Tools (see page 4)

INSTRUCTIONS

5 strands braided 2–2–1

Strands 1–4: For each strand load copper wire with 70 red bugles. Crochet chain, adding bead every stitch. For strand 5, load wire alternating 5 bugle beads, 1 clear crystal bead; repeat 11 times, ending with 5 bugle beads. Crochet chain, adding bead every stitch.

BRAIDING

Strands will be approx. 18" before braiding. Make 2 pairs with the red bead strands. Place strand 5 on the right and braid together so that the clear beads "pop" up in the center of the braid (see Braiding, page 7).

FINISHING

Attach finishing beads, jump rings, and clasp (see Finishing, page 8).

Aubergine

By Jacqui Harris
Finished necklace 1"x15"

MATERIALS

340 purple iridescent beads
11 rose quartz beads
15 yards of 28 gauge gold wire
Size H (5.00mm) aluminum crochet hook or size needed to obtain gauge of 4 chains = 1"
2 barrel beads
2 jump rings
Clasp
Tools (see page 4)

INSTRUCTIONS

5 strands braided 2–2–1

Strands 1–4: For each strand load wire with 70 bluish-purple beads. Crochet chain, adding bead every stitch. For strand 5, load wire alternating 5 purple beads, and 1 rose quartz bead; repeat 11 times, ending with 5 purple beads. Crochet chain, adding bead every stitch.

BRAIDING

Strands will be approximately 18" before braiding. Make 2 pairs with the red bead strands. Place strand 5 on the right and braid together so that the rose quartz beads "pop" up in the center of the braid (see Braiding, page 7).

FINISHING

Attach finishing beads, jump rings, and clasp (see Finishing, page 8).

Aqua Dream

By Basha Kooler
Finished necklace 1½"x28"

MATERIALS

(Beads are all crystal faceted except for silver beads)
22 small clear beads
43 small lavender beads
30 small aqua beads
30 small green beads
120 small silver beads
7 medium (8mm) blue beads
7 large (10mm) clear beads
7 ex-large (12mm) blue beads
38 yards of 26 gauge silver wire
Size H (5.00mm) aluminum crochet hook or size
needed to obtain gauge of 4 chains = 1"
2 barrel beads
2 jump rings
Heavy clasp
Tools (see page 4)

INSTRUCTIONS

9 strands braided 3–3–3

Strands 1–5: Crochet silver wire until each strand measures approx. 30". For strand 6 load the wire in the following sequence: small clear bead, small lavender bead, medium blue bead, small lavender bead, small clear bead, small lavender bead, ex-large blue bead, small lavender bead, small clear bead, small lavender bead, large clear bead, small lavender bead. Repeat 7 times, ending with small clear bead, small lavender bead. Crochet chain, adding bead to every stitch. Strands 7–8: For each strand load wire with 2 small silver beads, 1 small aqua bead, 2 small crystal beads, 1 small green bead, repeating 10 times. Crochet chain, adding bead every other stitch. Strand 9: Load strand with 2 small silver beads, 1 small aqua bead, 2 small crystal beads, 1 small green bead, repeating 20 times. Crochet chain, adding bead every stitch.

BRAIDING

Strands will be approx. 30" before braiding. Divide strands into 3 sections (section 1 = strands 1–3, section 2 = strands 4–6, section 3 = strands 7–9). Braid together the 3 strands in each section. With section 2 in the middle and section 3 on the right, braid the three sections together so that the large and medium blue beads "pop" up in the center of the braid (see Braiding, page 7).

FINISHING

Attach finishing beads, jump rings, and clasp (see Finishing, page 8).

Black and White Ball

By Jacqui Harris
Finished necklace 1"x16"

MATERIALS

356 black hex beads
148 (2mm) pearls
11 (8mm) pearls
15 yards of 28 gauge black wire
Size H (5.00mm) aluminum crochet hook or size needed to obtain gauge of 4 chains = 1"
2 barrel beads
2 jump rings
Clasp
Tools (see page 4)

INSTRUCTIONS

5 strands braided 1–2–2

Strands 1–2: For each strand load black wire with 74 black hex beads. Crochet chain, adding bead every stitch. Strands 3–4: For each strand load wire, alternating 74 black hex beads and 74 (2mm) pearls. Crochet chain, adding both a hex bead and pearl to each stitch. Strand 5: Load wire with 5 hex beads and 1 (8mm) pearl, repeating 11 times and ending with 5 black hex beads. Crochet chain, adding bead every stitch.

BRAIDING

Strands will be approximately 18" before braiding. Divide the 5 strands into 3 sections (section 1 = strand 5, section 2 = strands 1 and 3, section 3 = strands 2 and 4). Braid together with section 1 on the left, so that the large pearls "pop" into the center of the braid (see Braiding, page 7).

FINISHING

Attach finishing beads, jump rings, and clasp (see Finishing, page 8).

The Lariat

By Jacqui Harris
Finished necklace ¼"x44"

MATERIALS

83 (3mm) pearls
82 square aqua beads
2 round blue faceted crystal beads
2 large aqua crystal briolettes
8 yards of 28 gauge silver wire
Size H (5.00mm) aluminum crochet hook or size needed to obtain gauge of 4 chain = 1"
Tools (see page 4)

INSTRUCTIONS

Long strand for use as belt or lariat
Load silver wire, alternating pearls and square aqua beads and ending with a pearl. Leave a 4" wire tail on each end of strand for later adding the round blue bead and briolette Crochet chain, adding bead every stitch.

FINISHING

Thread one end of the wire with a pearl, a blue crystal bead, and a large aqua briolette, then thread the wire back through the blue crystal bead and pearl. Twist the wire several times between the blue bead and the briolette to center and secure the briolette and pearl, then cut the excess wire.

VARIATIONS

The variations here are just designs that don't quite fit into the previous categories. Think of all the different avenues you could take with each technique! Here are just a few of the variations possible.

The Grapevine

By Jacqui Harris
Finished necklace 1"x16"

MATERIALS

108 amethyst nuggets
10 yards of 28 gauge gold wire
Size H (5.00mm) aluminum crochet hook or
size needed to obtain gauge of 4 chains = 1"
2 barrel beads
2 jump rings
Clasp
Tools (see page 4)

INSTRUCTIONS

3 strands braided 1–1–1

Strands 1–3: For each strand load with 36 amethyst nuggets. Crochet chain, adding nugget every other stitch.

BRAIDING

Strands will be approx. 18" before braiding. Before braiding hold each end of the finished strand and give a hard tug. This will flatten the stitches. Braid the 3 strands together (see Braiding, page 7). Bend the wires at the top and along the bottom to give a more open and lacy appearance. Scrunch and fold the wire in places where it needs to hold the shape.

FINISHING

Attach finishing beads, jump rings, and clasp (see Finishing, page 8).

The Egyptian

By Jacqui Harris
Finished necklace ¾"x24"

MATERIALS

62 (6mm) yellow jade beads
90 golden raspberry triangle beads
248 raspberry seed beads
10 yards of 28 gauge magenta wire
Size H (5.00mm) crochet hook or size
needed to obtain gauge of 4 chains = 1"
2 barrel beads
2 jump rings
2 earring wires
5 two-inch head pins
1 three-hole dangle charm
Clasp
Tools (see page 4)

INSTRUCTIONS

3 short strands braided 1–1–1. Repeat to make two "bracelets" and attach with dangle charm at center of necklace. Shown with matching earrings.

Strands 1–4: For each strand load magenta wire, alternating golden raspberry triangle, yellow jade bead. Repeat 12 times, ending with golden raspberry triangle. Crochet chain, adding bead every other stitch. Strands 5–6: For each strand load wire, starting with 4 seed beads. Then load 1 golden triangle bead, 8 seed beads. Repeat 12 times, ending with a golden raspberry triangle then 4 seed beads. Crochet chain, adding beads in every stitch as follows: 4 seed beads, golden raspberry triangle, 4 seed beads, 4 seed beads, golden raspberry triangle etc. to end of strand.

BRAIDING

Strands will be approx. 10" before braiding. Divide 6 strands into 2 sections (section 1 = strands 1, 2 and 5, section 2 = strands 3, 4 and 6). Braid each section together and twist ends just 2 times (see Braiding, page 7). Attach one end of each braid through the single hole at the top of the 3-hole dangle charm. Thread wire ends back through larger beads and snip ends to secure. Load three head pins with beads as shown in photo and make loops to attach to the 3-hole charm.

FINISHING

Attach finishing beads, jump rings, and clasp (see Finishing, page 8).

EARRINGS

Load two head pins with beads as shown in the photo and attach to earring wires with a loop to secure.

Resources

Most products used to create the designs in this book are available at your local craft retailer. For specialty supplies or assistance in locating a retailer, consult the companies below.

The Beadery
P.O. Box 178
Hope Valley, RI 02832
401-539-2432
fax 401-539-2598
www.thebeadery.com

Mode Int'l, Inc.
1572 61st St.
Brooklyn, NY 11219
718-259-9224
fax 718-259-9090
www.modebeads.com

KOOLER DESIGN STUDIO BOOKS

Produced By:
Kooler Design Studio • 399 Taylor Blvd., Ste. 104 Pleasant Hill, CA 94523 • kds@koolerdesign.com•
Creative Director, Donna Kooler • Editor, Judy Swager
Writer/Photo Stylist/Book Designer, Basha Kooler
Graphic Designer/Illustrator, Maria Rodriguez •
Photographer, Dianne Woods

Published By:
LEISURE ARTS
the art of everyday living

PRINTED WITH SOYINK

Made in U.S.A.

ISBN 1-60140-019-5